WELLINGTON S...

UK and France

Sue Graves

Nelson

Contents

The United Kingdom

The United Kingdom is made up of four countries. The four countries are England, Scotland, Wales and Northern Ireland.

The capital city is London.

The United Kingdom

The United Kingdom is 244,000 square kilometres in area.

The people of the United Kingdom

usually speak English

use pounds sterling for money

France

France is a much bigger country than the United Kingdom.

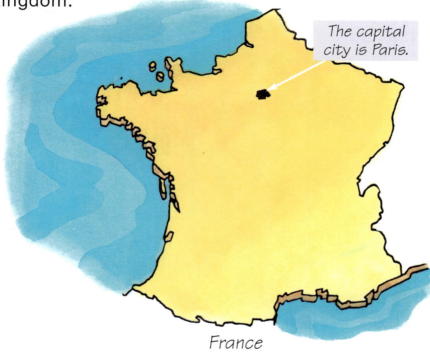

The capital city is Paris.

France

It is over 551,000 square kilometres in area.
This means that France is more than twice the size of the United Kingdom.

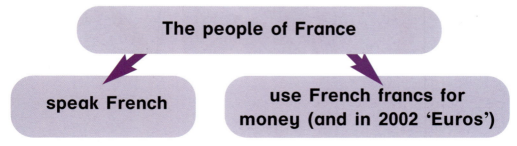

The people of France

speak French

use French francs for money (and in 2002 'Euros')

The Flags

The Union Jack

The United Kingdom's flag is called the Union Jack.

The Union Jack

The Union Jack is made up of three flags from three of the countries in the United Kingdom: England, Scotland and Ireland. Each flag has a different saint's cross on it.

St George's cross (England) *St Andrew's cross (Scotland)* *St Patrick's cross (Ireland)*

The Tricolore

The French flag is red, white and blue. It is called the Tricolore.

The French word 'tricolore' means that the flag has three colours.

The Tricolore

The Tricolore dates back to when France first became a republic in 1792.

Tricolore = three colours

Capital Cities

London

London is the capital city of the United Kingdom.
It is on the banks of the River Thames.

It is one of the biggest cities in the world.
More than 6.5 million people live there.

There are lots of things to see in London.

London bus   Beefeater Guard   Guards outside
Buckingham Palace

There are lots of places to visit, too.

Paris

Paris is the capital city of France.
It is on the banks of the River Seine.
It is also one of the biggest cities in the world.
More than 9 million people live there.
There are lots of things to see in Paris.

French policeman

Street cafés

The Left Bank

There are lots of places to visit, too.

Food and Drink

The United Kingdom has a wide
variety of foods. Some places in the United Kingdom
have famous foods and dishes named after them.

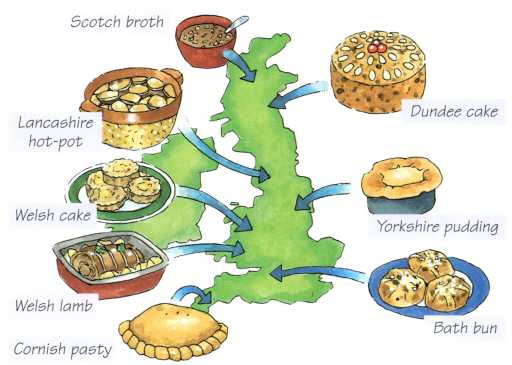

Scotch broth

Dundee cake

Lancashire
hot-pot

Welsh cake

Yorkshire pudding

Welsh lamb

Bath bun

Cornish pasty

The United Kingdom is also
famous for its cheeses.

Cheddar

Stilton

Red Leicester

*Some famous cheeses from
the United Kingdom*

France also has a wide variety of foods.
Some places in France have famous foods
named after them.

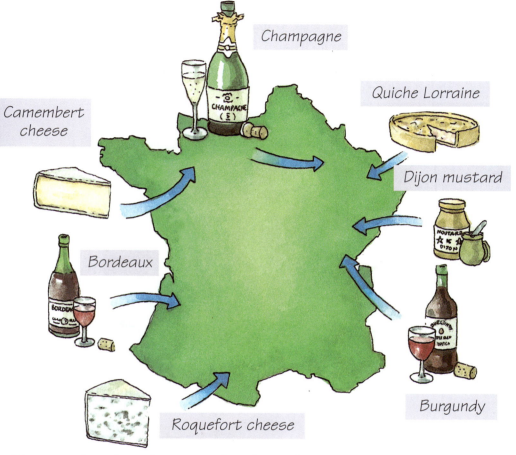

Champagne

Quiche Lorraine

Camembert cheese

Dijon mustard

Bordeaux

Burgundy

Roquefort cheese

France is also famous for its wines.
Wine is made from grapes.
Different places in France grow different sorts of
grapes that make different sorts of wines.
Some wines are named after the places where its
grapes are grown.

Breakfast

In the United Kingdom, people eat a
wide variety of food for breakfast.
Some people like to eat a full English breakfast or a
bowl of Scottish porridge.

Full English breakfast

Scottish porridge

But many people in the United Kingdom just like to
have cereal, toast and marmalade and a cup of
tea or coffee.

The French do not have a wide variety of food for breakfast. They usually eat 'baguettes' or 'croissants'.
These are eaten with butter and jam.

They buy fresh 'baguettes' and 'croissants' every day.

Some children eat 'pain au chocolat'. 'Pain au chocolat' is like a small bread roll with chocolate in the middle.

Many people in France like to drink coffee with breakfast.

Croissant

Pain au chocolat = bread with chocolate in the middle
Baguette = a stick of French bread
Croissant = Breakfast roll

Education

Schools

In the United Kingdom, children start school when they are five years old.

Many children go to state schools. Parents do not pay fees to send their children to these schools.

Some children go to private schools. Parents have to pay fees to send their children to these schools.

Children go to a primary school for six years.

A primary school

Children go to a secondary school when they are eleven years old.

A secondary school

French children start school at six years old.

Most children go to state schools.

There are some private schools, too. Most of the private schools belong to the Roman Catholic Church.

French children at primary school

French children stay at primary school until they are eleven. Then they go to a secondary school.

At fifteen, some children go to a lycee to take exams to get into university. Other children train for a job.

A lycee

lycee = a school for 16-18 year-olds

The School Day

In the United Kingdom, children have to go to school, each day, from Monday to Friday. The school day starts at 9 a.m. Most schools have an hour for lunch, from midday until one o'clock.

1 hour

Most children have to wear school uniforms, like these.

Some schools wear very unusual uniforms.

Primary school uniform

Christ Hospital School

In France, the school day begins at 8.30 a.m.
The children usually have two hours for lunch.

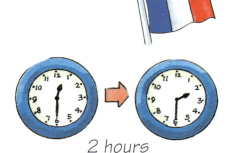

2 hours

Many French children do not go to school on Wednesday. They often like to play sport on Wednesday morning.

But they do have to go to school on Saturday morning.
Most French children do not wear a school uniform.

French classroom

Sport

People in the United Kingdom enjoy lots of sports.

One of the most popular sports is tennis. Another very popular sport is football. Many people like to watch football and tennis matches.

A football match

Many people like to take part in sport, too. These are some of the sports that they play.

jogging

rugby

tennis

cycling

riding

hockey

swimming

football

The French also enjoy sport. The most popular sports are football and cycling. The French have a special bike race called the Tour de France.

This bike race goes all around France.
The race is about 4,800 km long. This is about 3,000 miles.

The Tour de France

The French also like to play a game called Boules. Boules is like the English game of bowls. The balls used in the game are made of metal.

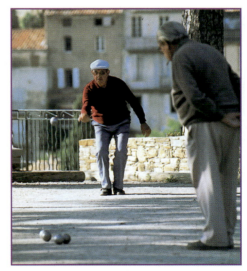

Boules

Tour de France = the name of a bicycle race around France

boules = bowls

Celebrations

Birthdays

Children in the United Kingdom like to celebrate their birthdays.
Some people get cards and presents from their families on their birthdays.

Some people celebrate by having a birthday party.

Saints' Days

Many French people like to celebrate their birthdays, too. They also get cards and presents.

Bon Anniversaire!

But some French people celebrate another day as well. They celebrate their saint's day or their 'name day'. If your name is Peter, you would celebrate Saint Peter's day.
On your saint's day you would be given a small present or perhaps have a small cake.
It's just like having another birthday.

Bon Anniversaire = Happy Birthday

Special Days and Fireworks!

People celebrate special days with parties and fireworks.
In the United Kingdom, people like to have firework parties on 'Guy Fawkes' night.

Guy Fawkes

Every 5th November, people have bonfire parties and fireworks to remind them of Guy Fawkes and the Gunpowder Plot of 1605.

The French like to celebrate special days, too. A very special day is Bastille Day on 14th July.

Bastille Day marks the start of the French Revolution in 1789 when the poor stormed the Bastille Prison in Paris. The poor were angry that the rich were wasting money on wars, when they were starving.

The Storming of the Bastille

France became a republic in 1792. Bastille Day is always marked with parties and lots of fireworks.

Glossary

croissant – a sort of bread roll

fees – sums of money paid for a service

gunpowder – material that will explode

lycee – type of school in France

porridge – cooked oatmeal

revolution – an uprising against a government

republic – a country run only by a government elected by the people. There is no royal family.

saint – someone who is very holy

university – a place where a person studies to get a degree

variety – a mixture

wine – a drink made from grapes

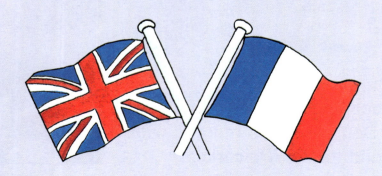